Jim Blank

Social Security for the Suddenly Single

SOCIAL SECURITY RETIREMENT AND SURVIVOR'S BENEFITS FOR DIVORCEES

Social Security for the Suddenly Single

By Jim Blankenship, CFP®, EA

ISBN 978-1979585583 / 197958558X

Use of the words "Social Security", "Social Security Account", "Social Security System" or "Social Security Administration" in this work should not be in any way interpreted or construed as approval, endorsement or authorization by the Social Security Administration, the Centers for Medicare and Medicaid Services, or the Department of Health and Human Services, or that the author has some connection with or authorization from the Social Security Administration, the Centers for Medicare and Medicaid Services, or the Department of Health and Human Services. It must be understood that all specific facts and rules explained in this book are freely available from the Social Security Administration.

Every effort has been made to ensure this publication is as accurate and complete as possible. However, no representations or warranties are made with respect to the accuracy or completeness of the contents of this book. It is not the intent of this publication or its author to provide professional tax, investment or legal advice. The strategies contained herein may not be suitable for your situation. You should consult with a professional where appropriate. This publication should only be used as a general guideline and not as the ultimate source of information regarding Social Security.

Requests for permission or further information should be directed to the author via email at Jim@BlankenshipFinancial.com.

About the author

Jim Blankenship is a financial planner based in New Berlin, Illinois. Through his Fee-Only financial planning practice, Jim provides unbiased financial advice to individuals from all walks of life.

Jim Blankenship, CFP®, EA

Jim@BlankenshipFinancial.com

Dedication

This book is dedicated to my wife Nancy. She is the loving voice of reason who helps me to remember to take a breath every once in a while. I couldn't do any of this without her.

Praise for "Social Security for the Suddenly Single"

With Social Security for the Suddenly Single, Jim Blankenship has created a well-explained cheat code for maximizing your Social Security benefits after divorce. This easy-to-read guide offers fully-researched answers to the question of how to make sure you get all the Social Security benefits you're entitled to. Blankenship steers you through the complex process of applying for Social Security benefits with a sure hand and a dash of humor.

- Emily Guy Birken, author of "The 5 Years Before You Retire"

If you're divorced and anywhere near Social Security age, then Jim's book is required reading! He takes a tangled web of rules and breaks them down into simple explanations and real-life examples. Armed with that knowledge, you can make decisions that could mean thousands more in benefits every year.

- Kathleen Campbell, Campbell Financial Partners, LLC

Jim Blankenship is the 'go to guy' for Social Security questions for many in the financial planning community. His books are on my bookshelf, and should be on the shelf of every planner or consumer.

- Eric Korbitz, CPA/PFS, CFP®, Korbitz Financial Planning

A great resource that provides a very targeted audience with exactly what they need to know.

- Garry Good, CFP®, Good Financial Advisors

Jim shines a light on complicated Social Security topics. A great resource for professionals and lay people.

- Michael Timmerman, CFP®, Timmerman Financial Planning

Other books by Jim Blankenship

A Social Security Owner's Manual

An IRA Owner's Manual

Acknowledgements

"My best friend is the one who brings out the best in me." – Henry Ford

I have been blessed with a good number of colleagues in the financial industry who I call my friends. These friends have helped me in uncountable ways throughout the years, providing advice, feedback, guidance and support in my efforts. In turn, I have, where possible, done my best to return the favor. But I always feel like I'm indebted, such is the giving nature of these friends. To all of you, I give my gratitude and heartfelt thanks.

Specifically, for this book, I need to call out several people by name. Each had a hand in the final production, and without each of you this book would be incomprehensible drivel. Much thanks to Tom Nowak, Laura Seymour, David Barnett, Kathleen Campbell, Eric Korbitz, Shawn Koch, Garry Good, Michael Timmermann, and Roger Wohlner.

A very special mention of thanks goes to Joshua Giminez for his very thorough review, which added immeasurably to the readability of this book.

A humble and heartfelt "thank you!" to Russ Thornton, the nationally-known expert on women's financial issues, for writing the foreword.

Foreword

If you or someone you know is dealing with divorce, you know how life-altering the process can be.

Dealing with children, parents, in-laws, friends and your soon-to-be ex can make your head spin.

Beyond the dynamics of changing relationships are the emotions. One moment you're angry, then you're sad, then you're scared, and all of these emotions float on a strong current of stress and anxiety.

And if things weren't already challenging enough, in the midst of all this, you'll need to think about and make some important financial decisions. Decisions that could have a lasting impact on your lifestyle for the rest of your days.

You're likely familiar with some of the terminology commonly associated with divorce. Things like alimony, child support, division of assets, QDROs, and more.

But an important, yet often less discussed, component of your post-divorce financial plan is Social Security and its available benefits for those who have gone through a divorce.

In my work with people going through divorce, I've often encountered a lot of confusion regarding how Social Security might play a role in your financial planning. I've even encountered some family law attorneys who seem to know just enough to be dangerous when it comes to Social Security and your divorce.

And unfortunately, you might get a different answer every time you contact the Social Security Administration with questions.

Given this state of affairs, it makes a lot of sense to seek the assistance of a professional with both the experience and deep understanding of Social Security benefits and how they might apply to someone dealing with divorce.

However, if you prefer to first educate yourself and learn all the ins and out of Social Security divorce benefits, you're in luck.

The book you hold in your hands (physically or digitally), written by my friend and colleague, Jim Blankenship, CFP®, EA, is an enormously valuable tool as you work to equip yourself to make smarter, more informed financial planning decisions as you go through your divorce.

Are you eligible for spousal benefits once you're divorced?

- How much could your benefit be?
- When can you begin taking spousal benefits and how will this impact the amount you receive?
- What if you're divorced and your ex-spouse is deceased?
- What are the potential reductions to your benefits?
- And what strategies should you utilize to get the most out of your Social Security benefits?

The answers to all these questions and much more are covered thoroughly in this book; written in plain English, and explained throughout via stories and examples.

Looking back at all the clients I've worked with as they face divorce, I wish I'd had this book handy so I could have given them a copy.

Fortunately for you, this isn't just wishful thinking.

Read this book. Use it to formulate questions to ask your divorce attorney or other professional advisors.

One of the biggest challenges of divorce is "you don't know what you don't know."

Well, when it comes to Social Security and its relevance to your divorce, now you'll know.

I hope you'll enjoy Jim's book as much as I did.

Russ Thornton, CDFA
Wealthcare for Women

Table of Contents

Chapter 1: Introduction

It must be understood at the outset that as the author of this book I have no connection with or authorization from the Social Security Administration, the Centers for Medicare and Medicaid Services, or the Department of Health and Human Services. Use of the words "Social Security", "Social Security Account", "Social Security System" or "Social Security Administration" in this work should not in any way be interpreted or construed as approval, endorsement or authorization by the Social Security Administration, the Centers for Medicare and Medicaid Services, or the Department of Health and Human Services.

The facts in this publication are freely available from the Social Security Administration. The organization, interpretation, and explanation of these facts have been developed by the author through years of studying the facts and rules of the system. It is the organization, interpretation and explanations that provide the value in this work.

A significant and growing number of us have been there: after many years of wedded bliss, the marriage is over. It is now rather late in life to be uncertain about your future. It can be daunting (to say the least) to be on your own, no longer part of a couple. You're facing the future alone - you're suddenly single.

The secure retirement that you once looked forward to as you approached your 60's may now be in doubt. You were counting on the combination of both of your retirement incomes to get by in retirement. Maybe you didn't work outside the home while the kids were in school, or maybe it's just that your own retirement savings and benefits alone aren't going to be enough.

Or perhaps you worked in the private sector and earned a Social Security benefit of your own, but you'd like to delay drawing on your benefits as long as possible in order to maximize your income - but it's going to be pretty tight on the finances in the meantime.

All is not lost. As a divorcee you may be eligible for benefits based on your ex's earnings record. There are certain qualifications that you must meet, but as long as you meet those qualifications you may have access to additional benefits.

Case: Kim – an increase in benefits

Kim was married to Paul for 27 years. Paul and Kim had raised their three children and together they had planned for a modest retirement in their hometown, so they could be near the grandkids. The money Paul had set aside, along with his Social Security benefit, would provide them with plenty of income to live out their sunset years in comfort.

Unfortunately, Paul and Kim divorced, and after all was said and done, Kim was awarded half of Paul's 401(k) plan.

After meeting with her financial planner, Kim has discovered that the 401(k) money is only enough to provide her with about two-thirds of the income she needs to live on. She has already checked on her Social Security benefits – she worked part-time while the kids were in school – so her Social Security benefit will only amount to an additional $500 per month when she reaches 66, her planned retirement age.

Since Kim is now 62 years of age, she has a few years to catch up with savings. But how is she going to make up the more than $1,000 shortfall to her income in just four short years??

It turns out, the Social Security rules are written to help Kim in this situation. By virtue of the fact that Kim worked in a low-paying job while the kids were young, enabling Paul to earn a very high salary, Social Security has a way to give Kim a benefit to make up for her sacrifices.

By the time Kim reaches age 66, her Full Retirement Age (FRA), she is eligible for a Spousal Benefit based on Paul's earnings record - in the amount of $1,250 per month. This, along with her savings over the next few years, will give her even more than she originally thought she'd need to live on - enough to be able to provide some education gifts for her grandchildren.

Case: Sylvia – Survivor benefits

Sylvia was married to John for 12 years and their divorce was finalized in 1983. Sylvia married twice more during the 1990's, but neither of those marriages lasted more than a few years. John, who was 15 years older than Sylvia, passed away two years ago. Sylvia is now 62, and she's facing a forced retirement due to her declining health.

Sylvia worked as a legal assistant for most of her adult life. According to her Social Security statement she could have a retirement benefit of $1,800 per month if she can delay retirement until she reaches her FRA of age 66. The problem is that she can't wait that long due to her health situation.

Again, Social Security has a way to help Sylvia out in her circumstances. Sylvia is eligible for an ex-spouse's Survivor Benefit from Social Security based on John's record. Since John was receiving a Social Security benefit at his death, Sylvia is eligible for a benefit of $1,620 per month right now. This will suffice to help her delay her own benefit until she reaches age 68. At that point her own benefit will have grown to a total of $2,088 per month.

Wondering how this all works? Wondering if it might help you in your situation? Read on, we'll explain the details.

Basic Social Security Rules

Below are several rules that are important for you to understand about Social Security as a divorcee. You can review this list briefly for now, and then perhaps come back to it as you work your way through the rest of the book.

It's important to understand that "divorced" in this book refers to a legal dissolution of the marriage. Legal separation, estrangement, and other statuses that are not a legal dissolution do not apply.

All Benefits

- Filing for any benefit before your Full Retirement Age (FRA) will result in a reduction. (See the table in Chapter 3 for Full Retirement Age by year of birth for retirement benefits. See the table in Chapter 7 for Full Retirement Age for Survivor Benefits.)

- For every month after Full Retirement Age (up to age 70) that you delay filing for your own retirement benefit, you will accrue Delayed Retirement Credits, increasing your future retirement benefit when you do file for it.

- To be eligible for benefits based on your ex-spouse's record, you must have been married for at least 10 years before divorcing. This includes Spousal Benefits and Survivor Benefits.

- Filing for Spousal or Survivor Benefits based on your ex-spouse's record has no impact on your ex-spouse's benefit amount. Furthermore, your filing for Spousal or Survivor Benefits based on your ex-spouse's record will not impact the ability for your ex-spouse's current or future spouse to receive benefits.

- Filing for benefits based on your ex's record has no impact on Family Maximum benefit limitations for your ex and his or her other family members.
- Family Maximum limitations do not apply to any benefits you receive as an ex-spouse.
- Filing for any kind of benefits based on your ex-spouse's record can be done completely on your own. Your ex-spouse does not need to know you have filed, and you don't need to contact your ex-spouse in order to file for the benefits based on his or her record (see Chapter 9).

Your Own Benefits

- The earliest age you can receive retirement benefits is 62.
- Deemed filing applies if you are eligible for Spousal Benefits; these subsequent benefits will automatically begin as you become eligible for them (more explanation in Chapter 2).
- At age 70 your benefits will not increase by delaying any longer. It doesn't make sense to delay receipt of benefits later than age 70.

Spousal Benefits

- The earliest age you can receive Spousal Benefits is 62.

- To be eligible to file for Spousal Benefits based on your ex's record, you must be at least 62 years of age, your ex-spouse must be at least 62 years of age and either two years have passed since the divorce was finalized or your ex has started receiving Social Security benefits based on his or her own record.

- If you have remarried before age 62 and remain in the subsequent marriage, you will not be eligible for Spousal Benefits based on any previous marriage, unless you have remarried a previous spouse.

- If you remarry while collecting Spousal Benefits based on your ex-spouse's record, you will no longer receive those benefits (except in one special case – see Chapter 6 for details).

- If a subsequent marriage ends (by divorce or death) then you will again be eligible for Spousal Benefits based on the earlier marriage.

- The earliest age that you can file a Restricted Application for Spousal Benefits is your Full Retirement Age. (*only applies if born before 1954)

- As divorcees, both ex-spouses may be allowed to file a Restricted Application for Spousal Benefits (on their ex's record) upon reaching Full Retirement Age. (*only applies if born before 1954)

- If you have filed for your own benefit prior to Full Retirement Age and are therefore receiving a reduced benefit by filing early, when you file for the Spousal Benefit (assuming that amount is larger than your own) you will never receive the full 50% of your ex-spouse's Primary Insurance Amount (Chapter 6).

- There is no increase to Spousal Benefits if you delay filing beyond your Full Retirement Age so there is no reason to delay filing past FRA.
- If you were born in 1954 or later, the Restricted Application for Spousal Benefits only is not available to you. This means that when you file for a retirement benefit you will be deemed to have filed for all retirement benefits that you are eligible for at that time (see Chapter 2 for more information about Restricted Application).

Survivor Benefits

- The earliest age you can receive Survivor Benefits is 60 (or 50 if you are disabled).
- If you have remarried before age 60, you will not be eligible for Survivor Benefits based on a prior marriage, for as long as the current marriage lasts. As mentioned previously, if the subsequent marriage ends, your eligibility is restored.
- If you remarry after age 60, you will continue to have eligibility to receive Survivor Benefits based on an earlier ex-spouse or late spouse, as long as you otherwise are eligible for those benefits.

- If a subsequent marriage ends (by divorce or death) then you will again be eligible for Survivor Benefits based on the earlier marriage.
- There is no increase to Survivor Benefits if you delay filing beyond your Full Retirement Age.

Chapter 2: The Ground Rules

As someone who is suddenly single, you may be eligible for four different kinds of benefits:

Retirement benefits - This is the benefit based on *your* lifetime earnings from jobs where Social Security tax was withheld. You can begin this benefit as early as age 62 at a reduced benefit amount. You can also delay receipt of this benefit to as late as age 70, which can result in delay credits (increases) applied to your benefit.

Spousal Benefits - These benefits are based upon the earnings record of your spouse or ex-spouse. Spousal Benefits can enhance or replace your own benefit for a period of time or permanently if larger than your own benefit. This benefit is also available as early as age 62. At your Full Retirement Age, this benefit is maximized – meaning it will grow no larger if you wait to file past FRA.

Survivor Benefits - This benefit is based on the earnings record of your late ex-spouse and is available after his or her death. The Survivor Benefit is available as early as age 60, or age 50 if you are totally and permanently disabled. This benefit attains its maximum amount when you have reached Full Retirement Age (FRA).

<u>Parent's Benefits</u> - The Parent's Benefit is available to a member of a couple who is caring for a child (under age 16) of the couple. This benefit may be available to a divorcee as either a Survivor Benefit (if the other parent has died) or as a pre-FRA unreduced Spousal Benefit. This benefit does not change with your age – but it ceases when the child reaches age 16 or you reach FRA.

We'll explain each type of benefit more completely in subsequent chapters. But first let's go over some more foundational information and definitions.

Full Retirement Age

Full Retirement Age (FRA) is the age at which you can receive a Social Security retirement benefit equal to your Primary Insurance Amount (PIA). Your PIA is calculated from a weighted average of your lifetime earnings, which we'll cover shortly. Full Retirement Age was originally 65 when Social Security began. However, it has increased in the past several years. For folks born between 1946 and 1954, the FRA is 66. Beginning with a birth year of 1955, the FRA increases by year of birth to a (current) maximum of 67 if born in 1960 or later.

If you were born after 1954, your Full Retirement Age (FRA) will be two months greater than age 66 for each year after 1954, to a maximum of age 67. For example, if you were born in 1957, this is three years after 1954, so two months for each year equals six months (2 x 3 = 6). Therefore, your Full Retirement Age is 66 years and six months if born in 1957. For folks born in 1960 or later, the FRA is currently capped at 67 years of age:

Full Retirement Age

Year of Birth	FRA
1943-1954	66
1955	66 and 2 months
1956	66 and 4 months
1957	66 and 6 months
1958	66 and 8 months
1959	66 and 10 months
1960 or later	67

Source: Social Security Administration

Note: persons born on January 1 of any year should refer to the FRA for the previous year.

Primary Insurance Amount

The Primary Insurance Amount (PIA) is the most important figure for calculating Social Security benefit amounts. The PIA is the basis for many calculations - your own benefit, the benefits of others (spousal and dependents' benefits) as well as benefits for your survivors.

It gets pretty complicated, but below is a brief description of the process of determining your PIA:

Social Security records your earnings over your lifetime, indexing the annual amounts for inflation. This way your earnings early in your career are adjusted to account for the effect of inflation.

The highest 35 years of indexed earnings over your career are averaged to determine your Average Indexed Monthly Earnings (AIME). If you've had fewer than 35 years of earnings or years when your earnings were very low, these low or zero years are included in the calculation. This has the effect of reducing the overall AIME.

Your Social Security retirement benefit isn't simply an average of your earnings (that would be too easy). There is a formula applied to the AIME, breaking it into 3 parts called "bend points".

For someone reaching age 62 in 2017, the first bend point is from $0 to $885; the second bend point is the amount between $885 and $5,336; and the third bend point is any of the AIME that is greater than $5,336. In 2018 the first bend point is $896 and the second bend point is $5,399. Anything above $5,399 is the third point.

The figures for the bend points change every year, and the bend points that apply to you are the ones that coincide with the year you reach (or reached) age 62.

The first bend point is multiplied by 90%; the second by 32%; and the third by 15%. These three results are then added together to produce your Primary Insurance Amount, or PIA.

Case: Cynthia's PIA

Cynthia, age 62, has had Average Indexed Monthly Earnings (AIME) over her career in the amount of $6,000. Running this through the formula using the 2017 figures, here is how it works:

90% of $885 = $796.50
32% of ($5,336 - $885 = $4,451) = $1,424.32
15% of ($6,000 - 5,336 = $664) = $99.60

Adding these three together we have:

$796.50 + $1,424.32 + $99.60 = $2,320.42.

This result is then rounded down to $2,320.40 – this is Cynthia's PIA. If Cynthia files for benefits at exactly her Full Retirement Age of 66 years and 2 months, her benefit will be $2,320.40 per month. Cost of Living Adjustments (COLAs) will apply between today and Cynthia's age 66 and 2 months, so the benefit will be higher as those COLAs are added.

Case: Charles' PIA

For another example, Charles, also age 62, has AIME of $3,500 per month. Inputting this average to the formula works out like this:

90% of $885 = $796.50
32% of ($3,500 - $885 = $2,615) = $836.80
15% of $0 = $0 (since Charles' AIME of $3,500 is less than $5,336)

Add the three together:

$796.50 + $836.80 + $0 = $1,633.30

This result is already rounded to $1,633.30. This is Charles' PIA.

Your PIA is equal to the amount of benefit that you will receive if you file for benefits at exactly your FRA. Depending on when you file for your benefit, the amount you receive could be more, less, or exactly the same as your PIA (plus the applicable Cost of Living Adjustments).

Reduction to Benefits

If you file for benefits prior to your FRA, your benefit will be reduced. This part (as with most Social Security calculations) is also a bit complicated. The reduction for early filing is not equal for all years. For the nearest 3 years before FRA, the reduction is 5/9% per month. Therefore, if you file exactly 36 months before FRA, the total reduction is 20% (5/9% times 36 = 20%).

For any months greater than 36 before FRA, the additional reduction is 5/12% per month, for a total of 5% per full year (5/12% times 12 = 5%).

The table on the following pages shows the rate of reduction for filing by month relative to FRA:

Months before FRA	Reduction from PIA
0	0% - your benefit is equal to PIA
1	-5/9% (or -0.5556%)
2	-1 1/9% (or -1.1111%)
3	-1 2/3% (or -1.6667%)
4	-2 2/9% (or -2.2222%)
5	-2 7/9% (or -2.7778%)
6	-3 1/3% (or -3.3333%)
7	-3 8/9% (or -3.8889%)
8	-4 4/9% (or -4.4444%)
9	-5%
10	-5 5/9% (or -5.5556%)
11	-6 1/9% (or -6.1111%)
12	-6 2/3% (or -6.6667%)
13	-7 2/9% (or -7.2222%)
14	-7 7/9% (or -7.7778%)
15	-8 1/3% (or -8.3333%)
16	-8 8/9% (or -8.8889%)
17	-9 4/9% (or -9.4444%)
18	-10%
19	-10 5/9% (or -10.5556%)
20	-11 1/9% (or -11.1111%)
21	-11 2/3% (or -11.6667%)
22	-12 2/9% (or -12.2222%)
23	-12 7/9% (or -12.7778%)
24	-13 1/3% (or -13.3333%)
25	-13 8/9% (or -13.8889%)
26	-14 4/9% (or -14.4444%)
27	-15%
28	-15 5/9% (or -15.5556%)
29	-16 1/9% (or -16.1111%)
30	-16 2/3% (or -16.6667%)

Months before FRA	Reduction from PIA
31	-17 2/9% (or -17.2222%)
32	-17 7/9% (or -17.7778%)
33	-18 1/3% (or -18.3333%)
34	-18 8/9% (or -18.8889%)
35	-19 4/9% (or -19.4444%)
36	-20%
37	-20 5/12% (or -20.4167%)
38	-20 5/6% (or -20.8333%)
39	-21 1/4% (or -21.25%)
40	-21 2/3% (or -21.6667%)
41	-22 1/12% (or -22.0833%)
42	-22 1/2% (or -22.5%)
43	-22 11/12% (or -22.9167%)
44	-23 1/3% (or -23.3333%)
45	-23 3/4% (or -23.75%)
46	-24 1/6% (or -24.1667%)
47	-24 7/12% (or -24.5833%)
48	-25%
49	-25 5/12% (or -25.4167%)
50	-25 5/6% (or -25.8333%)
51	-26 1/4% (or -26.25%)
52	-26 2/3% (or -26.6667%)
53	-27 1/12% (or -27.0833%)
54	-27 1/2% (or -27.5%)
55	-27 11/12% (or -27.9167%)
56	-28 1/3% (or -28.3333%)
57	-28 3/4% (or -28.75%)
58	-29 1/6% (or -29.16667%)
59	-29 7/12% (or -29.5833%)
60	-30%

Case: Cynthia's Benefit Calculation

Cynthia, with a PIA of $2,320.40, decides to file for her own retirement benefit to begin two months after her 63rd birthday. This is exactly 36 months before her FRA of 66 years, 2 months. Looking at the chart, we see that filing 36 months before FRA results in a reduction of 20% from Cynthia's PIA:

100% minus 20% = 80%
80% times $2,320.40 = $1,856.32

Cynthia will begin receiving a reduced monthly benefit of $1,856.30 at her age 63 years and two months (remember, benefits are always rounded down to the nearest dime).

Case: Charles' Benefit Calculation

Charles waits until his age 64 years and 10 months to begin his retirement benefits. This is 16 months before his Full Retirement Age (which is 66 years, 2 months, same as Cynthia's). His PIA of $1,633.30 is reduced by 8.8889% according to the table:

100% minus 8.8889% = 91.1111%
91.1111% times $1,633.30 = $1,488.12

Therefore, Charles' reduced monthly benefit beginning at his age of 64 years and 10 months will be $1,488.10 (rounded down).

Increase

On the other hand, when you delay filing for your own Social Security benefit past your Full Retirement Age (FRA) you earn Delayed Retirement Credits, or DRCs. These DRCs have been at various rates over the years, but the current rate is 8% per year, or 2/3% for every month of delay. This figure has been in place for quite some time and is not expected to change in the near future.

The following table illustrates the increases for delay credits:

Months after FRA	Increase added to PIA
0	0 (benefit is equal to your PIA)
1	+2/3% (or +0.6667%)
2	+1 1/3% (or +1.3333%)
3	2%
4	+2 2/3% (or +2.6667%)
5	+3 1/3% (or +3.3333%)
6	4%
7	+4 2/3% (or +4.6667%)
8	+5 1/3% (or +5.3333%)
9	6%
10	+6 2/3% (or +6.6667%)
11	+7 1/3% (or +7.3333%)
12	8%
13	+8 2/3% (or +8.6667%)
14	+9 1/3% (or +9.3333%)
15	10%
16	+10 2/3% (or +10.6667%)
17	+11 1/3% (or +11.3333%)
18	12%
19	+12 2/3% (or +12.6667%)
20	+13 1/3% (or +13.3333%)
21	14%
22	+14 2/3% (or +14.6667%)
23	+15 1/3% (or +15.3333%)
24	16%

Months after FRA	Increase added to PIA
25	+16 2/3% (or +16.6667%)
26	+17 1/3% (or +17.3333%)
27	18%
28	+18 2/3% (or +18.6667%)
29	+19 1/3% (or +19.3333%)
30	20%
31	+20 2/3% (or +20.6667%)
32	+21 1/3% (or +21.3333%)
33	22%
34	+22 2/3% (or +22.6667%)
35	+23 1/3% (or +23.3333%)
36	24%
37	+24 2/3% (or +24.6667%)
38	+25 1/3% (or +25.3333%)
39	26%
40	+26 2/3% (or +26.6667%)
41	+27 1/3% (or +27.3333%)
42	28%
43	+28 2/3% (or +28.6667%)
44	+29 1/3% (or +29.3333%)
45	30%
46	+30 2/3% (or +30.6667%)
47	+31 1/3% (or +31.3333%)
48	32%

Case: Robert's Benefit Calculation

Robert has a PIA of $1,500, and he's planning to file for his benefit at age 68 years and 4 months. This is a delay of 28 months after his FRA of age 66. When we look at the table, we see that his delay of 28 months will result in an increase of 18.6667% to his PIA:

100% + 18.6667% = 118.6667% times $1,500 = $1,780

Robert's benefit at his age 68 years and 4 months will then be $1,780 due to the delay credits.

Case: Laura's Benefit Calculation

Laura has a PIA of $1,850, and she wants to wait until she reaches age 70 to begin receiving benefits. Delaying to age 70 will maximize her benefit. This is a delay of 48 months since her FRA is age 66. This delay results in a 32% increase to her benefit:

132% times $1,850 = $2,442

At age 70 Laura will receive a monthly benefit of $2,442 due to the delay credits of 32%. This is an annual increase of over $7,000!

Deemed Filing

Deemed Filing is a rule that applies when an individual is simultaneously eligible for his or her own retirement benefit and a Spousal Benefit. If eligible for both types of benefit, filing for either type of benefit results in a completed filing for both benefits at the same time. **If you were born in 1954 or later, Deemed Filing applies to you at any age.** If born before 1954, Deemed Filing only applies when you are under Full Retirement Age.

Case: Debra, born in 1956

Debra, who divorced Tom 3 years ago, is eligible for a benefit of $500 at FRA based on her own work record. In addition, Debra is also eligible for a Spousal Benefit which would be $1,300 based on Tom's record if received when she reaches FRA.

Born in 1956, Debra won't be eligible for the Spousal Benefit when she reaches age 62 in 2018. Tom is four years younger than Debra, and therefore he will not be 62 for four more years. Debra can file for her own benefit when she reaches age 62, and the overall reduction to benefits will be $125. Therefore, she could receive $375 per month in benefits at this age. Then when Tom is 62 years old, Debra will be 66 which will allow her to receive the spousal *excess benefit* in full (without reduction).

Filing early for her own benefit doesn't come without consequences. When Debra files for the Spousal Benefit at FRA, the resulting monthly benefit she receives will not be the full $1,300 Spousal Benefit. Her overall benefit will be reduced since she filed for her own benefit early. The reduction of $125 per month will follow her when she files for the Spousal Benefit. She will receive $1,175 per month if she files for the Spousal Benefit at her FRA. The spousal *excess benefit* is calculated by subtracting Debra's PIA ($500) from the full Spousal Benefit ($1,300). The $800 result is then added to Debra's reduced benefit from filing early: $800 + $375 = $1,175.

It's important to note that, although Debra is eligible for both benefits, she effectively will receive only the result of her reduced benefit added to the *excess* Spousal Benefit. The two total benefits are not added together – only the excess is added.

Case: Karen, born in 1955

In slightly different circumstances, Edward and Karen were married for 15 years and divorced 6 years ago. Edward is a year older than Karen. Edward's PIA is $2,600 while Karen's PIA is $1,000. In this case since Karen was born in 1955, she would not be allowed to split up the benefits like Debra did. Since it has been more than two years since the divorce, and Edward is over age 62, Karen is eligible for the Spousal Benefit upon reaching age 62 herself.

When Karen is 62 she will be simultaneously eligible for two benefits: a Spousal Benefit and her own retirement benefit. Deemed Filing will impact Karen if she files for her own benefit at any age (she was born after 1954). When she files for either benefit, Karen is deemed to have filed for both benefits which she is eligible for at that age. The result (if Karen files at age 62) would be a composite benefit equal to 35% of

Edward's benefit, or $910. This is effectively the larger benefit of the two benefits she is eligible to receive.

If Deemed Filing applies, you are required to file for and accept all available benefits upon your filing. If at some point later in your life you become eligible for a Spousal Benefit that is larger, you are deemed to have filed for that benefit as soon as you are eligible.

Case: Leslie, born in 1955

Leslie is 62 and her ex-husband Dale is 61. Leslie could file for her own benefit at age 62 and accept the reduced benefit based on her own record. Then, a year later when Dale reaches age 62, Leslie will be deemed to have filed for the Spousal Benefit based on Dale's record. In this case, both benefits are reduced since Leslie has effectively filed for both benefits prior to her FRA. Leslie does not have to take any action. Deemed Filing caused her to start receiving the Spousal Benefit immediately when she becomes eligible for it, upon Dale reaching age 62.

However, if Leslie delays filing for any benefits until her FRA or older, although Deemed Filing still applies to her, she is effectively eligible to receive the largest of the two *unreduced* benefits.

Born before 1954

If you were born before 1954 and you are younger than FRA and eligible for a Spousal Benefit, Deemed Filing applies to you. Deemed Filing requires you to file for both your own benefit and the Spousal Benefits to which you are eligible, just the same as folks born in 1954 or later.

However, if you are at or older than FRA and were born before 1954, you have the option of splitting up your own benefit from the Spousal Benefit. This is known as a Restricted Application for Spousal Benefits, and we'll cover that process in the next section.

When you file for benefits before FRA, there will be reductions to your benefits, as we described earlier. But there can be other penalties for filing before FRA as well. One of these is Deemed Filing.

If you file for benefits prior to Full Retirement Age and you are also eligible to receive a Spousal Benefit (more on this in Chapter 5) you are required (deemed) to file for both benefits for which you are eligible.

Why is this important, you may ask?

In some circumstances you might wish to only file for the Spousal Benefit early, then delay filing for your own benefit until a later date. **This is known as a Restricted Application for Spousal Benefits – and it's only available for folks who were born before 1954.**

Restricted Application for Spousal Benefits (only if born before 1954)

Restricted Application for Spousal Benefits is a special method of applying for Social Security benefits. You must be at least Full Retirement Age (FRA) to file a Restricted Application. In addition, you must have been born before 1954. The law changed in 2015, eliminating this option, and grandfathering the option for folks born before 1954.

This is how it works: Instead of filing for all available benefits, you separate the Spousal Benefit from your own benefit. By doing so, you collect only the Spousal Benefit while delaying your own benefit until a later date. When delaying your own benefit beyond FRA, you earn Delayed Retirement Credits (DRCs) for every month that you delay, and at age 70 the DRC increase is maximized. When you file a Restricted Application for Spousal Benefits, you receive the Spousal Benefit (unreduced, because you are at or older than FRA). You can then wait to file for your own benefit at a later date when the DRCs have been applied to it.

Case: Donna's Restricted Application

For example: Donna's PIA is $1,000, and Steven's PIA is $1,500. Donna and Steven were married for 19 years and have been divorced for 7 years. Both Donna and Steven are currently 65 years old. If Donna waits until she is at Full Retirement Age of 66 she can file a Restricted Application for Spousal Benefits – which provides her with a Spousal Benefit equal to 50% of Steven's PIA, or $750 per month. Donna can then delay filing for her own benefit until a later age, as late as age 70. By delaying her own benefit, Donna accrues an 8% increase to her benefit for every year of delay. If Donna chooses to file for her own benefit at age 68 for example, her own benefit would have grown to $1,160 per month. Waiting until age 70 would increase her benefit to $1,320!

Filing a Restricted Application for Spousal Benefits has no impact on your own benefit, other than the fact that you are allowed to delay receipt of your own benefit until later. In other words, there is no downside to your future benefits by filing a Restricted Application for Spousal Benefits.

Chapter 3: Age Requirements

The minimum age at which you can receive Social Security benefits based on your own record is 62. The same age applies to Spousal Benefits based on your ex-spouse's record.

The minimum age at which you can file for a Survivor Benefit is 60, unless you are permanently disabled, in which case the minimum age is 50.

There is no minimum age for receiving a mother's or father's Survivor Benefit (when caring for a child under age 16), but the maximum age to receive this benefit is your own Full Retirement Age, or FRA. At that age, the mother's or father's benefit will convert to a Survivor's Benefit (as a spouse of the deceased).

The minimum age for receiving a mother's or father's Spousal Benefit as a divorcee is age 62, and the maximum is FRA. We'll cover the parent's benefits in greater detail in Chapter 7.

There is also a minimum age that your ex-spouse must achieve in order for you to be eligible for Spousal Benefits: your ex must be at least 62 years of age.

In addition, one of the following two conditions must be met for you to be eligible for Spousal Benefits:

- your ex-spouse must have filed for his or her own benefits; or

- two years have passed since the divorce was finalized.

This two-year wait enables what is known as "independent entitlement" to Spousal Benefits.

Independent entitlement means that you are entitled to the benefit regardless of your ex-spouse's filing status. When you are at least the minimum age (62), two years have passed since the divorce, and the ex is at least age 62, there is no requirement that the ex has filed for benefits in order for you to be entitled to the spousal benefit.

On the succeeding pages we'll go over the unique factors that apply to your Social Security benefits at various ages – age 62, Full Retirement Age, and age 70.

At Age 62

When you are 62 years of age you are eligible to file for Social Security benefits based on your earnings history. However, at that age the benefit that you will receive, both now and for the rest of your life, will be reduced. If your Full Retirement Age is 66 (meaning you were born between 1946 and 1954) the benefit will be reduced to as little as 75% of the amount you'd receive if you wait until 66 (your FRA).

The problem with starting benefits at the earliest age is that you are limiting the amount of monthly benefits you'll receive (possibly for the rest of your life). But timing can work in your favor at this stage: If you aren't yet entitled (or independently entitled, see above) to a Spousal Benefit, you could file for your own benefit early, and then wait until as late FRA and file for the full 50% Spousal Benefit (minus the early filing factor). This will only work if the Spousal Benefit is greater than what your full benefit would be at your Full Retirement Age. In addition, if your ex-spouse files for his benefit at some point prior to your FRA (assuming 2 years have not passed since the divorce was finalized), you will be deemed to have filed for the ex-Spouse Benefit at that time, with no further delay. (See Deemed Filing in Chapter 2.)

Case: Simone

Let's go through an example to illustrate:

Simone was married to Roger for 20 years. They divorced when both were 61 years old. Simone's Primary Insurance Amount (PIA) - the amount of benefit that she could receive at age 66 - is $800. Roger's PIA is $2,600.

When Simone reaches age 62 she has the option of filing for her own benefit immediately. Since Roger has not yet filed for his benefit and it has been less than 2 years since the divorce was finalized, Simone is only currently eligible for her own benefit. The benefit that Simone receives at age 62 will be reduced by 25%, to $600, since she's filing early.

Later, at Simone's age 63 (when 2 years have passed since the divorce) she is deemed to have filed for the Spousal "excess" Benefit based on Roger's record.

This excess benefit will be available to her since more than two years have passed since the divorce. (Incidentally, if Roger filed for his own benefit at any time before two years had passed, this would have deemed Simone to automatically have filed for her Spousal Benefits at that time.) The excess Spousal Benefit is calculated by subtracting Simone's PIA from 50% of Roger's PIA. The calculation would look like this:

Roger's PIA ($2,600) times 50% ($1,300) minus Simone's PIA ($800) equals $500.

So the maximum excess Spousal Benefit that Simone can receive is $500, which is added to her own benefit for a total benefit of $1,100.

However, since Simone is only 63 years of age when she becomes entitled to the Spousal Benefit, the excess Spousal Benefit is also reduced (since she's under FRA). Assuming she's exactly 63 years old, the Spousal Benefit at maximum would be 38.75% of

Roger's PIA. Running through the calculation as before:

Roger's PIA ($2,600) times 38.75% ($1,007.50) minus Simone's PIA ($800) equals $207.50.

Therefore, at age 63 the maximum excess Spousal Benefit that Simone could receive is $207.50, which is added to her own reduced benefit for a total benefit of $807.50.

The only way that Simone could receive the total Spousal Benefit of $1,300 is if she delays filing for either benefit until she reaches FRA. Otherwise, since she filed for her own benefit early, she will be deemed to have filed for Spousal Benefits as of the earlier of 1) Roger's filing for his own benefit; or 2) two years after their divorce was finalized.

Lastly, between age 62 and Full Retirement Age (FRA) there is a limit to the amount of income from a job or self-employment that you can earn before your Social Security benefits are affected. We'll go over this in Chapter 4, Reductions.

At FRA – age 66 (up to 67)

When you reach Full Retirement Age (FRA) you are eligible for your full, unreduced retirement benefit. This amount is equal to the Primary Insurance Amount (PIA; calculation details in Chapter 2). You could also be eligible for a full 50% of your ex-spouse's PIA as a Spousal Benefit when you reach FRA.

A note about the semantics: I use the word "also" above - meaning that you could receive the Spousal Benefit separately, via a Restricted Application if born before 1954. Or you could file for all available benefits, meaning you would effectively receive the larger of the two. If you choose to receive the Spousal Benefit alone (via Restricted Application) you can delay your own benefit until a later date and accrue delay credits to increase your future benefit.

Case: William

For example, William and Susan were married for 15 years and have been divorced for 10 years. William is due a benefit based on his own record in the amount of $1,500 when he reaches FRA later this year. William could also be eligible for a Spousal Benefit at his FRA in the amount of $1,000. In order to receive this benefit, William will forgo receiving his own benefit for a few years. Then he will file a Restricted Application for Spousal Benefits only (since he was born before 1954). Then he can receive the $1,000 Spousal Benefit until he reaches age 70, at which point his own benefit will have grown to $1,980.

Case: Amy

On the other hand, there's the case of Jonathan and Amy, married for 26 years, divorced for two. Amy is due a benefit at FRA in the amount of $900 per month. The Spousal Benefit based on Jonathan's record will amount to $1,200 per month. Even at the maximum delay credits, Amy's benefit can only increase to $1,188. So there is no need for Amy to file a Restricted Application - she'll just file for all available benefits at her FRA and effectively receive the larger of the two.

Additionally, there is no gain by delaying receipt of Spousal Benefits (or ex-Spousal Benefits) past FRA if you are eligible for them at that age. **The maximum amount available is 50% of your ex's PIA, which is allowed at your FRA. No point in delaying filing for this benefit past your FRA.**

The same holds true for Survivor Benefits - once you've reached FRA the Survivor Benefit will not increase beyond that amount available at that age.

We'll cover Survivor Benefits and the calculations later.

Another feature of reaching FRA – the Earnings Limits are eliminated. In other words, you can earn as much as you wish after reaching Full Retirement Age and your benefits will not be reduced as they are for earlier ages. See Chapter 4 for more details on Earnings Limits.

At age 70

Once you've reached age 70 you are at the maximum amount of benefit based on your own record. Delayed Retirement Credits (DRCs) stop accruing at this point. The maximum DRC is a 32% increase to your PIA. This applies if your FRA is 66 and you delay until age 70. With 4 full years of delay at 8% per year, your DRC increase is 32%.

On the other hand, if your FRA is 67, this only leaves 3 years between FRA and age 70 to earn DRCs - so 24% is the most your DRC can be.

It is for these reasons that there is really no point at all to delaying receipt of Social Security benefits after age 70, unless for some reason you're not eligible for benefits at that point.

At Any Age

Once you've filed for benefits at any age, if you're continuing to work, your lifetime earnings record is updated every year. If the most-recently-recorded year's earnings are greater than one of your "top 35" years earlier in your career, your PIA will be recalculated based on the new AIME. This could occur in cases where there were zero-earnings years or very low earnings earlier in your career.

In addition, there is a special rule that can cause reductions to your benefits, called the Windfall Elimination Provision (WEP). WEP impacts folks who have earned a pension from a job that was not subject to Social Security taxes. We'll go over WEP more completely in the next chapter, but for now just know that earning income in a Social Security-covered job can help to reduce or eliminate the impact of WEP later on when you are receiving Social Security benefits.

Chapter 4: Reductions

In addition to the reductions for filing earlier than Full Retirement Age (FRA) that we covered earlier, there are a few other provisions that may cause a reduction to your benefits.

Specifically, there are Earnings Limits that can reduce your benefit before you reach FRA. In addition, there are two types of rules that can reduce your benefits: Windfall Elimination Provision (WEP) and Government Pension Offset (GPO). WEP and/or GPO may apply if you are receiving a pension from a governmental entity or a foreign pension plan that was not covered by Social Security.

We'll cover each type of reduction in the following pages.

Earnings Limits

When you are receiving Social Security benefits of any kind, there is a limit to the wages you can earn if you are under Full Retirement Age. If your earned income* is greater than $16,920 (2017 figure), for every $2 over this limit, $1 will be withheld from your Social Security benefit. In 2018 the limit is $17,040

In the calendar year that you reach FRA (but before the month you reach FRA), the earnings limit is more liberal. The limit for 2017 is $3,740 per month ($3,780/mo in 2018), and when you breach that limit, the reduction to benefits is $1 for every $3 in excess earnings.

After you have reached FRA, these earnings limits do not apply at all – you can earn as much as you like and your Social Security benefit will not be reduced.

The earnings limits apply to all types of Social Security benefits – your own, Spousal Benefits, Survivor Benefits, and Parent's Benefits.

Case: Thomas

Thomas, age 63, will earn $20,000 this year, which is $3,080 more than the limit. Since Thomas is receiving a Social Security benefit and he's under FRA, a total of $1,540 in benefits will be withheld – 50% of the over-earned amount of $3,080.

Thomas is receiving a Social Security benefit of $1,070 per month, so this means that 2 months' worth of his benefits will be withheld, typically in the first two months of the following calendar year. (The excess withheld will be applied to the following calendar year.)

This can come as a surprise if you've been receiving the full benefit and the earnings test is applied at the beginning of the following year. Due to the withheld benefits Thomas won't receive a check for two months!

In the year that you reach FRA (but before you actually turn 66 or whatever your FRA is) the earnings test is much more liberal: the limit for 2017 is $44,880 ($45,360 in 2018). The other difference is that for every $3 over the limit, $1 is withheld from your benefits. The rule is actually applied on a monthly basis, at the rate of $3,740 per month ($3,780 in 2018) for the partial year.

After you reach FRA, you'll get an adjustment to your benefit for the withheld checks. From our example, Thomas had two months' worth of benefits withheld during the 3 years before the year he reached FRA. When Thomas turns 66, he will receive credit for the months of withheld benefits. At FRA his benefit will be adjusted as if he had filed 6 months (3 years times 2 months) later than he actually filed. So, if Thomas originally filed at age 62, his benefit will be adjusted as if he filed at 62 years and 6 months. This results in an increase of 2.5% to his benefit.

***What earnings are counted?** Only earnings from employment or self-employment are counted toward these earnings limits. There is a rather long list of income types that do not count toward the earnings test – here's a brief rundown of non-counted earnings (only for Social Security earnings test, not for income taxation):

- deferred income (based on services performed before becoming entitled to Social Security benefits)
- court awards, including back-pay from an employer
- disability insurance payments
- pensions
- retirement pay
- real estate rental income (if not considered self-employment, i.e., the individual did not materially participate in the production of the income)
- interest and dividends
- capital gains
- worker's compensation or unemployment benefits
- jury duty pay
- reimbursed travel or moving expenses as an employee
- royalties - only exempted in the year you will reach FRA, otherwise royalties are counted toward the earnings test

Windfall Elimination Provision (WEP)

Another rule that may reduce your benefits is the Windfall Elimination Provision, or WEP. WEP applies only to your own benefit, not to Spousal, Survivor or Parent's Benefits.

WEP applies when you have worked in a job and earned wages that were not subject to Social Security taxes. Examples include federal, state, and local government jobs, many teaching jobs, as well as work in a foreign country that was not covered by Social Security (and which produces a pension from that work). If you've worked in a job that was not covered by Social Security, WEP could impact your benefits if you also worked in a job or jobs that were covered by Social Security.

WEP causes a reduction to your Primary Insurance Amount (PIA) by reducing the first bend point (covered in Chapter 2) by as much as 50%.

Case: Pam

Pam has worked as a teacher for most of her career, although she also worked during the summers at part-time jobs that were covered by Social Security. The part-time work has been enough to garner Pam a Social Security benefit. However, since her teaching salary was not covered by Social Security (she'll get a pension from her state teacher's retirement system), the WEP applies to her Social Security benefits by reducing her PIA.

Pam's PIA is $900 before the reduction for WEP. The WEP reduction is 50% of the first bend point, which in Pam's case is $826. So Pam's benefit is reduced by

$413, 50% of the first bend point. This means that her Social Security benefit will be reduced by $413 – to a final WEP-reduced amount of $487 per month.

There is a way that WEP impact can be reduced, and possibly eliminated altogether. If your earnings from Social Security-covered jobs has been "substantial" for more than 20 years, each year (greater than 20) of substantial Social Security-covered earnings will reduce the WEP impact by 10%.

"Substantial" earnings is a figure set by Social Security each year. For example, in 2017 earning at least $23,625 is considered "substantial". Following is a table that displays substantial earnings over the years:

Year	Substantial Earnings
1937-1954	$900
1955-1958	$1,050
1959-1965	$1,200
1966-1967	$1,650
1968-1971	$1,950
1972	$2,250
1973	$2,700
1974	$3,300
1975	$3,525
1976	$3,825
1977	$4,125
1978	$4,425
1979	$4,725
1980	$5,100
1981	$5,550
1982	$6,075
1983	$6,675
1984	$7,050
1985	$7,425
1986	$7,825
1987	$8,175
1988	$8,400
1989	$8,925
1990	$9,525
1991	$9,900
1992	$10,350
1993	$10,725
1994	$11,250
1995	$11,325
1996	$11,625
1997	$12,150
1998	$12,675
1999	$13,425
2000	$14,175
2001	$14,925
2002	$15,750
2003	$16,125
2004	$16,275
2005	$16,725
2006	$17,475
2007	$18,150
2008	$18,975
2009-2011	$19,800
2012	$20,475
2013	$21,075
2014	$21,750
2015	$22,050
2016	$22,050
2017	$23,625

Case: Sarah

Sarah worked for the state government for a portion of her career, but she worked in the private sector as an attorney for the majority of her working life. As a result of her work for the state, Sarah is eligible for a pension from the government. Sarah's earnings in the private sector, which were covered by Social Security, were substantial for 26 years (see table above).

When Sarah collects her pension from the state, her Social Security will be reduced but not as much as it would have had she not had substantial earnings for 26 years. Since Sarah has 6 years more than 20 in her "substantial" earnings record, the WEP impact will be reduced by 60%. The maximum amount of WEP impact for Sarah was to be $413 per month – with the 60% reduction, her WEP factor is reduced to only $165 per month.

It is possible to completely eliminate the impact of WEP. If Sarah had 30 years of substantial earnings, the WEP impact would be eliminated altogether. Likewise, if she continues working and accruing substantial earnings years (while collecting benefits), each year her benefit will be recalculated to include the additional substantial earnings year credit, reducing WEP until eliminated.

Government Pension Offset (GPO)

The other way that working for a governmental unit can impact Social Security benefits is called the Government Pension Offset, or GPO for short. This offset applies to Spousal Benefits or Survivor Benefits based on your spouse's or ex-spouse's earnings record.

When you have worked for a domestic (US) governmental unit, such as a state, federal or local government entity, or as a teacher in many states, and your earnings have not been covered by Social Security, GPO may impact your Spousal or Survivor Benefits. Two-thirds (2/3) of the amount of your pension will be subtracted from your Social Security Spousal or Survivor Benefit, potentially eliminating the Spousal or Survivor Benefit completely.

Unlike WEP, there is no way to earn your way out of the impact of GPO. Also, GPO decreases your actual benefit, not the PIA that is used to calculate the benefit.

Case: Kathleen

Kathleen worked as a teacher for her entire career, never working in Social Security-covered employment. Kathleen is divorced from Ronald, who only worked in Social Security-covered employment. When Kathleen retired at age 60, she started receiving a pension from her state's teacher's retirement system in the amount of $2,000 per month.

Having been married to Ronald for 27 years, once Kathleen reached age 62 she wanted to explore the Social Security Spousal Benefit option based on Richard's record. Richard is due a Social Security benefit of $2,200 when he reaches FRA. Since their divorce was more than 2 years ago, Kathleen is independently-entitled to apply for Spousal Benefits, regardless of whether Richard has filed for his own benefit.

Unfortunately, GPO will completely eliminate Kathleen's Spousal Benefit: 2/3 of her pension is $1,333.33, and the maximum Spousal Benefit based on Richard's record is $1,100. Subtracting $1,333.33 from $1,100 results in a negative number, so Kathleen is not eligible for a Spousal Benefit at all, due to the impact of GPO.

However, when Richard dies, Kathleen can be eligible for a reduced Survivor Benefit based on Richard's record. Richard started his Social Security benefits at age 66 in the amount of $2,200, and then he died two years later at age 68. Kathleen is also age 68.

GPO will reduce the Survivor Benefit available to Kathleen, but it will not eliminate the benefit. Kathleen's Survivor Benefit (before reduction) is $2,200, the same amount as Richard had been receiving when he died. Subtracting $1,333.33 (2/3 of Kathleen's pension) from the Survivor Benefit results in a monthly benefit of $866.67 per month for Kathleen.

Case: Noreen

Noreen worked a few years for her city's government, earning a pension of $1,100 upon her retirement. Noreen was married to Donald for 17 years before the divorce. Donald's PIA is $2,300. When Noreen reaches FRA she will be eligible for a reduced Spousal Benefit – calculated as follows:

2/3 of her pension is $733.33. Subtract that amount from the maximum Spousal Benefit (50% of Donald's PIA): $1,150 - $733.33 = $416.67. Additionally, upon Donald's death, Noreen could be eligible for a GPO-reduced Survivor Benefit of $1,566.67 ($2,300 minus $733.33 = $1,566.67).

Factors for Both GPO and WEP

It's important to note that the GPO and WEP are only applicable if you are receiving a pension from a government entity that is based on your own earnings that were not covered by Social Security taxation. If, for example, you are receiving a survivor's pension from a government entity based on your late spouse's employment, this survivor pension will not trigger GPO or WEP impact.

Also, the pension does not have to be a monthly annuity, as a "pension" is commonly thought of. If you have a retirement plan with the governmental entity that was a defined contribution-type plan (such as a 457 or 403(b) plan), WEP and/or GPO will still apply if the defined contribution plan is the **primary** retirement plan. If the 457 or 403(b) (defined contribution plan) is **supplemental** to a primary traditional pension plan, WEP and GPO will most likely not apply.

If there is a defined contribution plan that is the primary retirement plan, the Social Security Administration will convert the lump-sum amount of your savings plan into a monthly figure based on Social Security's actuarial tables to calculate the WEP or GPO reduction.

Chapter 5: Your Own Retirement Benefit

Your own Social Security retirement benefit is based on your life-long earnings record in jobs where Social Security taxes were withheld.

The earliest age that you are eligible for retirement benefits is 62. At this age your benefit will be reduced to the minimum amount. The way the reduction for filing early works is illustrated in Chapter 2.

The minimum benefit (received by filing at age 62) for a person with a Full Retirement Age (FRA) of 66 is 75% of his or her Primary Insurance Amount or PIA (see Chapter 2 for more information on the PIA). If your FRA is 67, the minimum benefit by filing at age 62 is 70% of the PIA.

On the other hand, if you delay receiving benefits to some point after your FRA, you will accrue an increase to your benefits known as a Delayed Retirement Credit or DRC. DRCs are also covered in Chapter 2. The maximum benefit for a person whose FRA 66 is 132% of PIA – and the maximum for a person whose FRA is 67 is 124% of PIA.

The retirement benefit is available to anyone who has worked in a Social Security-covered job for at least 40 quarters (10 years) earning the minimum amount in those quarters. For 2017 a "quarter of coverage" is credited to you for each quarter that you earn at least

$1,300 ($1,320 in 2018). This amount changes every year (due to inflation), and you can only earn 4 quarters per calendar year.

As discussed previously, filing early for your own benefit carries additional rules: not only is your benefit reduced, but you are also subject to earnings limits while you're younger than FRA, which may reduce your benefit. Plus, if you have filed for your own benefit before you achieve FRA and you're also eligible for Spousal Benefits, deemed filing will require that you file for all available benefits. This may take away some maximization options that you might have wanted to use later.

It seems counterintuitive, but often it makes a great deal of sense to use your savings (IRAs, 401k plans, etc.) or pensions earlier in order to delay filing for benefits based on your own record. By using these savings funds earlier you can maximize the amount of your Social Security benefit. The Social Security benefit has two factors that make it superior to other sources of retirement income: 1) maximum of 85% taxation (and possible exclusion from income); and 2) annual Cost of Living Adjustments.

Case: Sylvia

Sylvia is 65 years of age, and has been divorced from Kenneth for 16 years after their 20-year marriage. Sylvia is leaving the workforce due to declining health, and she has met with Social Security to file for Medicare. Her primary concern is running out of money in retirement.

Sylvia has a 401(k) plan with her soon-to-be former employer, which has about $40,000 in the account. She also has a pension coming to her upon her retirement, which will provide $10,000 per year, with no cost-of-living adjustments. Sylvia's annual expenses in retirement are expected to be around $20,000 per year, as her home is paid off, and her needs are quite simple.

When Sylvia met with the Social Security representative to file for Medicare, she was relating her situation with regard to her income concerns. The Social Security representative ran the numbers and told Sylvia that she could file for her retirement benefit right away and receive a benefit of $933 per month, or $11,200 per year. This is a bit more than Sylvia actually needs, and she was very tempted to take it.

The good news is that Sylvia had the card of a financial advisor who knew what questions to ask – and how to get the most from her available resources. Sylvia's advisor Laura recommended that Sylvia wait until reaching age 66 to file for any Social Security benefits. By doing so, at the very least, Sylvia will avoid a reduction from her PIA, which is $1,000 per month, or $12,000 per year.

This will require Sylvia to use $10,000 from her 401(k) plan – but there's more to the story. Laura encouraged Sylvia to find out more about her ex-husband Kenneth's earnings record with Social Security. Sylvia has had no contact with Kenneth for many years and doesn't even know where he lives these days.

With guidance from Laura, Sylvia gathered together her marriage certificate and divorce decree, along with Kenneth's Social Security number from an old tax return. Armed with this information, Sylvia was able to get an estimate of potential ex-Spouse Benefits based on Kenneth's record. Amazingly, the Spousal Benefit is $1,000 per month – exactly the same amount Sylvia would receive if she waited to file for her own benefit at FRA.

With the picture complete, Sylvia brought this information back to Laura, who recommended that Sylvia file a Restricted Application* for Spousal Benefits at her FRA (66), which would provide $1,000 per month. At this point Sylvia is bringing in more than she needs for her living expenses. After waiting until she reaches age 70, Sylvia's own retirement benefit will be maximized at $1,320 per month due to the delay credits earned by waiting.

This is an increase of more than $4,600 per year over the amount of benefit Sylvia could have received had she filed for benefits at age 65, which was her first instinct. Originally she was offered $933 per month ($11,196/year), and using the strategy outlined she can receive $1,320 per month ($15,840/year).

The outcome for Sylvia is that more than half of her income is subject to annual cost-of-living adjustments, and she's bringing in about 25% more than her living expenses (pension of $10,000 plus SS benefits of $15,840 equals $25,840 – against living expenses of $20,000). Plus, given that Kenneth is 8 years older, it's very likely that he'll die before her, so Sylvia may receive another increase to her benefits upon his death. (This increase at Kenneth's death is due to the way Survivor Benefits are calculated, which is a much more beneficial calculation. See Chapter 7 for more details on Survivor Benefits calculations.)

*It's important to note that Sylvia had the Restricted Application option available to her since she was born before 1954. If she was born in 1954 or later, the outcome would have been quite a bit different – she could still have delayed receipt of benefits until her FRA, but if she started benefits at that age she would not have the Restricted Application available. This means that either she would continue delaying all Social Security benefits while drawing on her 401(k) plan, or she could start benefits at FRA, in the amount of $1,000 per month.

If she delays benefits, her 401(k) plan may run out of money by the time she reaches age 69 – but in doing so, her Social Security benefit will have increased to $1,240 per month by that time. This is a permanent increase that will last for the rest of her life – or the rest of Kenneth's life, if he predeceases her.

In either case, whether Sylvia was born before 1954 or after, if Kenneth dies before Sylvia, she will be eligible for a Survivor Benefit equal to at least $2,000, Kenneth's PIA. More on Survivor Benefits in Chapter 7.

Chapter 6: Spousal Benefits

As a qualifying divorcee, you may be eligible for a Spousal Benefit based on your ex-spouse's earnings record as well.

This Spousal Benefit is (at a maximum) 50% of your ex-spouse's Primary Insurance Amount (PIA) - the amount of benefit that your ex would receive if he or she filed at exactly Full Retirement Age (FRA).

In order to be eligible for the Spousal Benefit based on your ex's earnings record, you must have been married to your ex-spouse for at least 10 years (no extra "combat pay" for sticking with it for a longer period of time, unfortunately!). In addition to the length of marriage test, your ex must be eligible for a retirement benefit. This means he or she must be at least age 62 and has earned the requisite 40 quarters of Social Security coverage.

Lastly, to file for the ex-Spouse Benefit you must be unmarried. You could have been remarried after the divorce, but in order to be eligible for the Spousal Benefit as a divorcee you must be currently unmarried. If you've been married and divorced more than once, you may be eligible for a Spousal Benefit based on more than one ex-spouse's record. You can switch and choose a more beneficial ex-spouse's record at any time, as long as you are eligible for those benefits by virtue of the length of the marriage and the ex's age.

Your ex-spouse does not have to be actively receiving benefits, as long as your divorce was finalized at least 2 years prior (and the ex is at least age 62). If the divorce was finalized less than 2 years ago, you will not be eligible for a Spousal Benefit until either your ex has applied for his or her own benefit, or two years have passed since the divorce.

Case: Anna and Steven

Anna and Steven, both age 62, were married for 17 years. Their divorce was finalized last week. Neither Anna nor Steven has filed for Social Security benefits. If Steven decides to file for his own benefit, he will not be eligible for a Spousal Benefit based on Anna's record – since Anna has not filed for her own benefit and the divorce has not been finalized for two years.

If Anna files for her own benefit, Steven would then be eligible for a Spousal Benefit. However, when Anna files, if it is after Steven has filed, she will be subject to "Deemed Filing", meaning that she will automatically file for all available benefits when she files for her own benefit (more on Deemed Filing in Chapter 2). So, if she wanted to delay filing for Spousal Benefits, she would have to delay her own benefit as well.

Case: Larry and Catherine

Larry and Catherine were married for 27 years and they divorced five years ago. Larry is now 65, and Catherine will reach age 62 later this year. When Catherine reaches age 62, she will be eligible to file for her own benefit and the Spousal Benefit based upon Larry's earnings record. In fact, since she's younger than FRA, deemed filing will apply if she files for any benefit at all, so she'll receive both benefits (effectively the larger of the two, both reduced by early filing) upon filing for her own benefit. Deemed filing applies here because Catherine is independently entitled to a Spousal Benefit based on Larry's record, regardless of whether he has filed for his own benefit. This is because two years have passed since the divorce was finalized.

If Larry waits until his FRA in one year, he will have the option of filing solely for Spousal Benefits (via a Restricted Application since he was born before 1954), while delaying his own benefit until a later date, as late as his own age 70. This is because Catherine is at least age 62, and the divorce was finalized more than two years before. Restricted Application is covered in more detail in Chapter 2.

Remarriage

You're only eligible to apply for Spousal Benefits based on your ex-spouse's record if you are currently unmarried. In most cases, if you are currently receiving a Spousal Benefit based on your ex-spouse's record, remarriage (to someone other than your ex) will eliminate your eligibility for those ex-spouse benefits.

There is one situation where this rule does not apply: If the person you are marrying is also collecting a Spousal Benefit, a Survivor's Benefit, or a parent's benefit for caring for a child under age 16, then both your own Spousal Benefit and your soon-to-be spouse's benefits will continue.

Case: Jane and Sheryl

Jane is divorced from Gerald. Jane has been receiving Spousal Benefits based on Gerald's record for the past couple of years. Jane is engaged to marry Sheryl. Sheryl's husband Ed died several years ago, and she has been collecting a widow's benefit (Survivor Benefit) based on Ed's record for a couple of years now.

Since Sheryl is receiving the Survivor Benefit based on Ed's record, the exception applies for Jane's ex-Spouse Benefit, and Jane will be eligible to continue receiving this benefit after the marriage. If Sheryl was not currently collecting the Survivor's Benefit (or one of the other noted benefits), Jane's ex-Spouse Benefit would end once her upcoming marriage starts.

One important factor here is that Jane and Sheryl are both *currently receiving* the benefits (in Social Security parlance, they are *entitled* to the benefits). If Jane was not currently receiving the ex-Spouse Benefit when she and Sheryl get married, she would not be allowed to start receiving the ex-Spouse Benefit based on Gerald's record while she and Sheryl are married.

Likewise, if Sheryl was not receiving the Survivor Benefit or one of the other noted benefits as of the date of Sheryl's and Jane's marriage, Jane's ex-Spouse Benefit would end when they get married.

Case: Jeffrey and Kathy

Jeffrey, age 60, and Kathy, age 63, are considering marriage. Kathy is divorced from Gregg, having been together for 23 years. The divorce occurred 4 years ago, and Kathy recently started receiving reduced Social Security benefits based on her own record in the amount of $900 per month. She also is receiving a Spousal Benefit increase to her own benefit (based on Gregg's record) in the amount of an additional $150 per month.

If Jeffrey and Kathy do get married, Kathy's Spousal Benefit increase of $150 based on Gregg's record will cease. Her total benefit at that time will be the $900 based on her own record. As long as she and Jeffrey are married, Kathy will not be eligible for the Spousal Benefit based on Gregg's record. She would eventually become eligible for a Spousal Benefit increase based on Jeffrey's record, but he will need to file for his benefit in order to enable this.

However, if Jeffrey and Kathy divorce or Jeffrey dies, Kathy's eligibility for the Spousal Benefit based on Gregg's record will be restored, as long as Gregg is still living. In the case of a divorce, if Jeffrey and Kathy were married for at least 10 years, Kathy would be eligible for the Spousal Benefit on either Jeffrey's or Gregg's record – whichever one is more beneficial for her. She can even choose one benefit first and then later change to the other if it is more advantageous.

Chapter 7: Survivor Benefits

If you were married to your ex for at least 10 years before your divorce, when your ex-spouse dies you may be eligible for a Survivor Benefit based on your ex's earnings record.

To be eligible for this Survivor Benefit, you must be at least age 60 (or age 50 if you are totally and permanently disabled). In addition, you must not have remarried prior to age 60. After age 60 you could remarry and still remain eligible for the Survivor Benefit. But if you remarry even one day before reaching age 60 your eligibility is suspended while the current marriage lasts. If the current marriage ends due to a subsequent divorce or the death of your current spouse, your eligibility for Survivor Benefits based on your ex-spouse's record is restored.

If there is more than one ex-spouse to whom you were married for at least 10 years, you are eligible to receive the highest of any of the applicable Survivor Benefits. You can actually switch between Survivor Benefits from one ex-spouse to another at any time that the other ex-spouse's record results in a higher Survivor Benefit for you. The same applies to any earlier spouse you may have been currently married to who died during the marriage, as long as the marriage lasted at least one year before the death of that particular spouse.

If you were re-married and your subsequent spouse died (for example), you will likely be eligible for Survivor Benefits based on your ex's record or your subsequent late spouse's record, whichever is more advantageous to you. You can also switch between late spouse (and late ex-spouse) Survivor Benefit records if the circumstances provide more benefits from another record.

If you file for any of these Survivor Benefits prior to reaching your FRA, there will be a reduction from the maximum amount of Survivor Benefit available to you. This is similar to the reductions that we reviewed earlier regarding your own benefit and the Spousal Benefit, but there are a few differences.

For one, the FRA table is slightly different for Survivor Benefits versus the FRA table for the other benefits.

Full Retirement Age (Survivor Benefits)

Year of Birth	FRA
1945-1956	66
1957	66 and 2 months
1958	66 and 4 months
1959	66 and 6 months
1960	66 and 8 months
1961	66 and 10 months
1962 or later	67

Source: Social Security Administration

Note: persons born on January 1 of any year should refer to the FRA for the previous year.

If you'll recall (or if you check back to the earlier table showing FRA for your own or Spousal Benefits) the years of birth for FRA of age 66 were 1943-1954. **The FRA for Survivor Benefits is two years later than the FRA for the other benefits.** This two-year difference applies across the board to all birth years.

Another difference for Survivor Benefits is that the minimum benefit is 71.5% of the base amount of Survivor Benefits, and the amount of decrease is ratably applied between age 60 and FRA. In other words, no matter when your FRA is, the minimum Survivor Benefit that you will receive is 71.5% of the base, and this reduction of 28.5% is applied evenly over the months before FRA.

If your FRA is 67, this means that each month before FRA results in a reduction of 0.3392% from the base amount. If your FRA is 66, the reduction per month is 0.3958%.

The last difference for the Survivor Benefit is in determining the "base" amount - and there are two ways that this can be determined, depending on whether the decedent (your late spouse or ex-spouse) was already receiving retirement benefits or not.

If the ex was not already receiving retirement benefits when he or she died, then the "base" amount is determined by the age of the decedent. If your late ex-spouse was at FRA or younger than FRA (on the first FRA table, not the Survivor Benefit FRA table), then the base is your late ex-spouse's Primary Insurance Amount (PIA). If he or she was older than FRA at death, then the base amount is whatever his or her retirement benefit amount would have been had he or she started collecting his or her own retirement benefits on the day of death.

On the other hand, if the late spouse or ex had already begun receiving retirement benefits by the date of his or her death, it gets even more complicated. In this case we need to get three figures to determine the "base":

1. The amount of retirement benefit that the decedent was actually receiving;
2. The product of 82.5% times the PIA of the decedent; and
3. The reduced benefit based on the PIA of the decedent and the survivor's age when filing.

These three amounts are listed from lowest to highest. Then the following determination is made: if #3 is less than either of the others (#1 & #2), then that amount (#3) is used for the calculations. If #3 is the greatest of the three amounts, then the larger of the other two amounts is the benefit amount used for the calculations. I realize that computation is very complex and convoluted, so here's a brief example:

Case: Jane

Jane is a surviving ex-spouse. Her ex-husband Dick had started receiving his retirement benefit earlier this year at age 62, just a few months before his death. Jane is now 64. Dick's PIA was $2,000, and since he started receiving his benefit at age 62, his benefit was reduced to $1,500.

So, we run our calculations to come up with the three figures:

1. $1,500 (actual benefit that Dick was receiving);
2. $1,650 (82.5% times Dick's PIA);
3. The reduced benefit based upon Dick's PIA and Jane's age, which calculates to 90.167% times $2,000, or $1,803

Arranging these figures from lowest to highest gives us 1,2,3. As described above, if #3 is the largest of the three figures, then the larger of the others is the actual benefit - so #2, $1,650, is the base amount of the Survivor Benefit that Jane is eligible for in these circumstances. This is the maximum amount of Survivor Benefit that Jane is allowed at her Survivor Benefit FRA.

If Jane starts receiving the Survivor Benefit at some point prior to her FRA, the reduction factor for her age will apply to the base amount that we calculated before. Jane is 64, and so we calculated the reduction factor for that age to be 90.167%. If Jane files for the Survivor Benefit now, her benefit would be 90.167% of $1,650, or $1,487.70 (always rounded down to the nearest dime).

As you can see, there is a wide range of benefit amounts that Jane could receive under various circumstances. These range from a low of $1,222.50 up to a maximum of $1,650.

Chapter 8: Parent's Benefits

There are a couple of ways that divorcees can collect benefits that depend on their status as a parent of a "child in care". A child in care is a child under age 16 in the care of the parent, or a child of any age who is mentally or physically disabled, provided the disability began before age 22. The child must be the child of the person whose Social Security record is used to determine the benefits.

As a married spouse, when you are younger than FRA and you have a qualifying child in care, you may be eligible for a parent's benefit if your spouse is receiving Social Security benefits. <u>This benefit is not available to a divorced spouse under age 62</u> – the child may continue receiving benefits based on his or her parent's record, but a divorced parent under age 62 cannot receive parents' benefits. Upon reaching age 62 if there is a child in care under age 16 who is receiving benefits based on the ex's record, an unreduced Spousal Benefit is available. If the child reaches age 16 and is not disabled, and the divorcee caring for the child is under FRA, the parents' (Spousal) benefit to the divorced spouse will cease. The divorcee could at this point switch to an age-reduced Spousal Benefit, or delay receipt of Spousal Benefits as usual.

Your child will also be eligible for a benefit of an equal amount (50%) until reaching age 18, or age 19 if a full-time student (not higher than grade 12 – high school senior).

Case: Linda and Amy

Linda, age 61, was married to James, age 63, for 25 years when they divorced. Linda and James have a daughter, Amy, who is 13 years old. James decides to file for his Social Security retirement benefit. Because James has filed, his daughter Amy is eligible for a benefit based on James' record. She will receive 50% of James' PIA (the amount he would have received had he waited until FRA to start benefits). Once she reaches age 62, Linda can receive a parent's benefit (unreduced Spousal Benefit) until Amy reaches age 16. This parent's benefit is also 50% of James' PIA. Amy can receive this benefit until she reaches age 18, or age 19 if she's a full-time (high school) student. If Amy is disabled, her benefit and Linda's benefit can continue beyond those ages.

Amy reaches age 16 before Linda reaches FRA, so there is a decision-point for Linda. She could either cease receiving benefits based on James' record altogether until she reaches FRA, or she could begin receiving a reduced Spousal Benefit at that time. This is available to her since she is eligible for Spousal Benefits (she's over age 62, James is over age 62 and James is collecting Social Security based on his record).

If she chooses to receive the reduced Spousal Benefit, deemed filing will apply, such that if her own (reduced) benefit is greater than the (reduced) Spousal

Benefit, she would only receive her own benefit and no Spousal Benefit would be available to her.

On the other hand, if Linda chooses to cease benefits at that point (prior to FRA, when Amy has reached age 16 and is not disabled), Linda has the option of waiting until FRA and filing a Restricted Application for Spousal Benefits (only if she was born before 1954). This way if Linda's own benefit might be larger than the Spousal Benefit at some point (with the accrual of delay credits) she is protecting that option for later.

If Linda was born in 1954 or later, she does not have the Restricted Application option available to her – so if she files for either benefit she cannot delay the other benefit.

Chapter 9: Strategies

As a divorcee, you have a few strategies that you can use to maximize benefits over your lifetime. For example, you might be eligible for a parent's benefit when your children are young, and then a different benefit when the kids reach age 16 or you reach FRA, either solely based on your ex's record or restricted to your ex's record and maximizing your own benefit via Delay Credits. Later in life you may have the option of switching over to a survivor benefit if your ex predeceases you.

How to Plan for Spousal Benefits Without Talking to the Ex

In order to be able to receive Spousal Benefits based on your ex-spouse's record, you'll need to provide information about your ex-spouse. You'll need to prove to the Social Security Administration (SSA) that you were married for the required number of years. You need to identify your ex-spouse, and you'll need to provide proof of the length of your marriage.

All of this can be simpler if you have ready access to your ex-spouse's information. But often after a divorce, communication with the ex presents more problems.

How Can You Plan?

Once you've determined that as a divorcee you are (or may be) eligible for a Spousal Benefit based on your ex's record. How can you plan? How can you determine what amount of Spousal Benefit you may have available?

Of course, a quick and easy way to know how much your Spousal Benefit might be is to ask your ex-spouse. He or she should know (or should be able to find out readily) the amount of Social Security benefits that he or she will have coming upon retirement.

But it's often not so easy – naturally, a byproduct of divorce is communications may be cut off, by either or both parties. Even if communicating is possible, it may be far from the desirable choice. The good news is that you don't have to do it that way. It is possible for you to go to the SSA office near you to find out on your own.

But wait a minute – you'd at least hope that the SSA folks won't simply hand out personal information to just anyone who darkens their threshold, right? I mean, you can't just walk in and ask for Social Security benefit information for another person's record without proving that you are entitled to access this information.

Of course, there is a certain amount of information that the SSA staff will not give you – your ex's Social Security number and address, for example. But if you prove your relationship to the ex – that is, if you can show evidence that you were married for the applicable 10 years or more, and that you are divorced – you can get some information from SSA for planning purposes.

This evidence that you must provide is in the form of a marriage license and a divorce decree. Both items must be the official records, not copies. Usually you can get these documents from the vital records office of the county where you were married and divorced, respectively. If these are different counties you'll need to contact each office separately to get the required documents. There will likely be a fee to get official copies of these documents.

In addition, if you don't have your ex's Social Security number, you will have to provide enough identifying information to ensure that the records requested are for the appropriate person, your ex. This identifying information includes full name, including maiden name if applicable, date of birth, place of birth, known addresses, parents' names and addresses, and possibly other information to correctly identify your ex.

If you have copies of old tax returns, this is a good place to get your ex's Social Security number! If you don't have copies of your old tax returns, you can request a copy from the IRS using Form 4506, Request for Transcript (for more information go to www.IRS.gov).

Once the record has been identified and your relationship to the individual is established, SSA may give you access to your ex's:

- **Primary Insurance Amount (PIA)** – for use in determining what your future Spousal and Survivor Benefits might be.
- **Earnings Record** – for use if you believe that the PIA may be incorrect due to incorrect information in the earnings record, to pursue a review of earnings record discrepancies.

Generally, with the information specified above these inquiries can be made over the telephone, although in certain situations a request must be made in person. If your request is not in person, you will likely need to fax or email your evidence documents.

Get Some Benefit Now, Get More Later

In this strategy, you must be at least at your Full Retirement Age (FRA, see Chapter 2) and eligible for a Spousal Benefit based on your ex's record. You also must be eligible for a benefit based on your own earnings record, and that benefit must either be larger or will grow to be larger than the Spousal Benefit at some point in the future.

Case: Rebecca

Rebecca is approaching age 66, her FRA. Rebecca and Terry divorced four years ago, and Terry started taking his Social Security benefit at his own age 66, two years ago. Terry's benefit at age 66, which is also his PIA, is $2,000 per month.

As Rebecca plans her benefit strategy, she takes note of the PIA that Terry has ($2,000), which means that at her FRA Rebecca could be eligible for a Spousal Benefit in the amount of $1,000. Rebecca went to the SocialSecurity.gov website to get her benefit information, and learned that her own benefit at age 66 will be $990 per month.

Given that her own benefit is just a bit less than the Spousal Benefit, it seems like all Rebecca can do at this point is file for the highest available benefit when she reaches FRA. But there's a catch to that – or rather, there is a benefit to planning this out and taking a slightly different approach.

When Rebecca reaches FRA she can file a Restricted Application for the Spousal Benefit alone – this means that she is ONLY filing for the Spousal Benefit, not for any benefit based on her own record. With the restricted application filing, Rebecca begins receiving the $1,000 per month in benefits based on Terry's record.

THEN, when Rebecca reaches age 70, she can now file for her own benefit, while that benefit has grown to $1,306.80 – an increase of 32% due to the delay credits.

If Rebecca didn't know about this beforehand, she might have just gone online and filed for her own benefit when she reached age 66, which would have eliminated the option of filing for a greater amount later.

It's important to note that Rebecca was eligible to use this strategy because:

1. Rebecca was at least her FRA
2. Rebecca was born before 1954
3. Her ex was at least age 62
4. Their marriage lasted at least 10 years
5. Their divorce was two years earlier OR Terry has filed for his retirement benefit
6. Rebecca had not filed for any Social Security benefit earlier (including Social Security disability)
7. Rebecca's own benefit was eventually going to be greater than the Spousal Benefit

Without all seven of those factors in place, the restricted application would not be available for Rebecca's situation.

Strategizing with Survivor Benefits

As a surviving divorced spouse, you have an opportunity to utilize some strategic moves that could result in increased benefits to you for your lifetime.

Because of the way Survivor Benefits work in conjunction with retirement benefits, all Social Security beneficiaries who are eligible for Survivor Benefits can use this strategy.

If you're over age 60 and you are eligible for a Survivor Benefit in addition to your own benefit, you have a decision to make. You can either start your own benefit at age 62 (or later) and then choose to file for the Survivor Benefit later on OR, you can file for the Survivor Benefit early, waiting to file for your own benefit until a later point.

Case: Gina

To illustrate, Gina and Ben were married for 20 years and divorced a few years ago. Ben died at the age of 67 after starting his retirement benefit at 66. Gina is 62 when Ben passes away. Ben's benefit when he died was $1,800 per month, and Gina has a benefit (based on her own record) of $1,200 per month if she waits until her FRA (66 years and 2 months).

At this point, Gina could start her own benefit (reduced for the early start) at the amount of 74.1667% of her PIA, or $890 per month. By doing so, she can receive this amount for the coming four years, delaying receipt of the Survivor Benefit. At her FRA for Survivor Benefits (age 66), Gina can start receiving the full amount of Ben's benefit amount, $1,800 per month.

On the other hand, Gina could start receiving the Survivor Benefit right away. It would be reduced to $1,458 per month. This would allow her to delay her own benefit until some later date.

Since at her FRA her own benefit would only be $1,200, it wouldn't make sense for her to switch to her own benefit then. But if she delays to any point past her own age 68 years and 10 months (32+ months' delay), she would be eligible for a larger benefit. In fact, if she delays to age 70, her own benefit will have grown to $1,568.

The second choice works out better for Gina in the long run. Even though the initial Survivor Benefit is significantly reduced, the eventual benefit she receives is much higher.

Divorcee Benefits Matrix

On page 85 you will find a matrix that describes the various benefits you have available to you as a divorcee.

To use this matrix, start at **1**, choosing your birth year. Then move to **2** and choose the age you wish to learn about available benefits. Now choose your length of marriage (**3**), and your ex-spouse's status (living or deceased) – **4**. Lastly, choose the appropriate column for **5**, whether or not you have a Child in Care under age 16.

Case: Bernadette

As an example, Bernadette was married to Robby for 17 years. Robby is still living, age 62, 2 years older than Bernadette. Robby has not begun collecting benefits at this point. The couple has no children, and they have been divorced for one year.

Bernadette is wondering about the earliest benefits she can receive from Social Security. She starts in column 1 with "Any Birth Year", and then reviews the second column. At her present age of 60, she sees that while Robby is still living she is not eligible for any benefits.

So she looks to the next row in the Age column (2) – indicating age 62 to FRA. Since her Step 3 value is that the Marriage lasted 10 years or longer, Bernadette next checks step 4 – Robby is still living, and not presently collecting benefits. However, by the time Bernadette reaches age 62, it will have been two years since the divorce. Because of this, Bernadette sees that she is (between the ages of 62 and her FRA) eligible for the larger of the reduced Spousal Benefit or her own reduced benefit.

Bernadette would also like to estimate what her benefit would be if she waits until her FRA or later to apply for benefits. Knowing what she knows from the previous exercise, she would just move down the table to the appropriate Step 1 value. Her birth year is 1957 so she chooses the row "1954 or later". This indicates that Bernadette will be eligible for the larger of her own benefit or the Spousal benefit – neither benefit is reduced since this estimate is assuming she's either at or older than FRA.

Lastly, Bernadette would like to check on what benefits she might be eligible for upon Robby's death. Moving to the right on the matrix to the set of columns indicating the ex-spouse is deceased, and since there is no Child in Care, Bernadette can review the various Survivor Benefit options that are available at various ages for her. At her present age (60) she would be eligible for a reduced Survivor Benefit if Robby were to die. At any age from 62 to FRA, she would be eligible for her choice of the reduced Survivor Benefit or her own reduced benefit. At or older than FRA, she has the same choice available, but neither benefit is reduced once she's reached FRA or older.

1 Birth Year	2 Age	Marriage Less than 10 years before divorce	Marriage 10 years or longer before divorce					
			Ex-Spouse is Living and Not Collecting Benefits	Ex-spouse is Living and Collecting Benefits		Ex-Spouse is deceased		4
				No Child in Care	Child in Care	No Child in Care	Child in Care	5
Any Birth Year	Under age 60	No Benefits	No Benefits	No Benefits	No Benefits	No Benefits	Parent's Benefit	
Any Birth Year	Age 60-61	No Benefits	No Benefits	No Benefits	No Benefits	Survivor Benefit (reduced)	Your Choice of: Parent's Benefit / Survivor Benefit (reduced)	
Any Birth Year	62-FRA	Your own benefits only	The Larger of: Spousal Benefits* (reduced) / Your own benefit (reduced)	The Larger of: Spousal Benefits (reduced) / Your own benefit (reduced)	Your Choice of: Spousal Benefits (unreduced) / Your own benefit (reduced)	Your Choice of: Survivor Benefit (reduced) / Your own Benefit (reduced)	Your Choice of: Parent's Benefit / Survivor Benefit (reduced) / Your own Benefit (reduced)	
1954 or later	FRA or Older	Your own benefits only	The Larger of: Spousal Benefits* (unreduced) / Your own benefit (unreduced or increased by DRC)	The Larger of: Spousal Benefits (unreduced) / Your own benefit (unreduced or increased by DRC)	The Larger of: Spousal Benefits (unreduced) / Your own benefit (unreduced or increased by DRC)	Your Choice of: Survivor Benefit (unreduced) / Your own Benefit (unreduced or increased by DRC)	Your Choice of: Survivor Benefit (unreduced) / Your own Benefit (unreduced or increased by DRC)	
1953 or before	FRA or Older	Your own benefits only	Your Choice of: Spousal Benefits* (unreduced) / Your own benefit (unreduced or increased by DRC)	Your Choice of: Spousal Benefits (unreduced) / Your own benefit (unreduced or increased by DRC)	Your Choice of: Spousal Benefits (unreduced) / Your own benefit (unreduced or increased by DRC)	Your Choice of: Survivor Benefit (unreduced) / Your own Benefit (unreduced or increased by DRC)	Your Choice of: Survivor Benefit (unreduced) / Your own Benefit (unreduced or increased by DRC)	

** if ex-spouse is at least age 62 and divorce was 2 or more years ago*

Acronyms

AIME – Average Indexed Monthly Earnings

AWI – Average Wage Index

COLA – Cost of Living Adjustment

DRC – Delayed Retirement Credits

EEA – Earliest Eligibility Age

F&S – File and Suspend

FMB – Family Maximum Benefit

FRA – Full Retirement Age

GPO – Government Pension Offset

NH – Number Holder

PIA – Primary Insurance Amount

SSA – Social Security Administration

WEP – Windfall Elimination Provision

Made in the USA
Lexington, KY
16 February 2018